FLUX

FLUX

JOE DENHAM

NIGHTWOOD EDITIONS

ROBERTS CREEK, BC
2003

Nightwood Editions
R.R. #22, 3692 Beach Ave.
Roberts Creek, BC
VON 2W2, Canada

Edited for the house by Silas White
Typesetting by Carleton Wilson

We gratefully acknowledge the support of the Canada Council for the Arts and the British Columbia Arts Council for our publishing program.

NATIONAL LIBRARY OF CANADA CATALOGUING IN PUBLICATION

Denham, Joe, 1975–
        Flux / Joe Denham.

Poems.
ISBN 0-88971-194-1

        I. Title.

PS8557.E54F58 2003   C811'.6   C2003-905245-1

for my family

CONTENTS

DOWSER

i.

The first time, walking at dusk alone
through fields of yarrow and thimble clover,
the wishbone willow branch twitched

then swung like a pendulum
downward, y-end oscillating: magnet
sucked to magnet. Startled, I

dropped the sudden divining rod,
let it fall from small fingers and plunge
like a pebble into a deep, dry well.

ii.

An omen? An answer? A calling
from hell? My child-mind
haunted by imaginings

in the dark: clairvoyant, unverifiable.
My phobia of closets and corners
incurable by homeopathy, herbalism, even

orthodox medicine. Insomnia's only remedy:
hypnotism by a bare sixty-watt bulb
stared into – eye strained – entered.

iii.

Took to sleeping under Perseus and Cassiopeia,
dream-body free to wander beyond
wall, rafter, window, roof.

The salt-brine air pungent
with ripe Himalayan blackberries
and the pine-scent of sap and porous cone

lulled me to sleep, quashing
my daemon's designs on hands
hypersensitive to water's purling drone.

iv.

This respite short-lived in midsummer's
dry season, September's southeasterlies
brought the dank scent of cobwebs, compost,

washed-up kelp. Damp
morning dew grew heavier
until October's first cold snap

frost-quilted my bed, forcing me back
indoors, my hand's sleep-flail
hungering for the hunt as-yet-unnamed.

v.

Dowser. Diviner. Water Witch.
But also *Dreamer. Lazy. Kook.*
Ill-prepared for a world bent into one

hook of excess, my largesse
dismissed as fraudulent, unfounded.
Took to drink and television to

placate the pulsing liminal pull
of untappable ore veins, flowing water
mains – the ineffable *hows* and *whys*.

vi.

Now? Offer proof. Or narrow the mind
to white sugar, neon signs. Tight
tendons and clenched masseters.

Pluck nose hairs and slouch
over work. Shovel and grunt.
Nothing to love or supplicate to but

the self. Flutter to exhaustion.
Cocoon my butterfly wings.
Come out caterpillar.

NIGHT HAUL, MORNING SET

NIGHT HAUL

I etch ephemeral sketches in flat, black water,
swirling the pike pole like a sparkler wand,
the steel spear tip igniting fairy-dust krill
as we drift in to haul up our catch.
An industrial gramophone, the hauler
churns a music of creak and moan
over the rumbling whine of diesel
and hydraulics, the echo of our exhaustion.
We sit astride the gunwale, hunched
and awing at the swooping arc of green
the line bends below the surface,
tugging the boat over the set –
till traps stream like marine comets
emerging from the depths in a burst of glow
and morphing back to bare utility
whatever beauty we'd begun to imagine.

BREAKFAST

Stiff as a crustacean's carapace
we cram into rain gear and stretch
on gloves to the auxiliary's muffled yodel
and the gargle of percolating coffee.
A quick cup and smoke on deck
with some *Nice to see your smashed-*
asshole face this mornin', then toque
and flashlight on, and climb down
into the forty-below-Celsius hold.
Bent into the boat's cramped belly
cold air clasps our lungs in a metallic
vice – crystallizes to ice upon inhale,
melts to mist with each exhale – as we
load totes down through the hole's
narrow mouth, feed it the frozen flesh
we caught and killed last night.

FO'C'SLE DREAMS

Too often working, or caught in the pincer
of a karma-charged crab. Last night
I crawled the sea floor, crustaceous. Clawed
through a maze of lost gear: rusting
traps, twisted snaps, line smothering coral.
Lured by the scent of fish feed on the tide
I climbed the limestone cliff it misted
down from; up trap-mesh, in through ring-tunnel.
As I lifted to the lip of the elastic-harnessed
bait cup hung above me
it was empty. That's when the darkness
shuddered. The trap dragged, then sprung
from the rock and sucked me upward,
my calcified body compressed by velocity,
water's weighted pressure. Eighty fathoms
hauled by the force of hydraulics to the surface.

We are ever-attentive to the sound
of the hauler. The line spinning
like an oiled chain through straight cogs
sets a rhythm we all move to
like a road-bike racer entranced
by the drivetrain's smooth song.
But when the line slips, steel plates worn
like overworked cog teeth, or tightens
and clicks like a stressed chain about to snap,
the metre falls off. We're moving too fast.
Ahead: a sharp switchback. Wet asphalt.
Test the brakes. Focus. Is every nut
and bolt secure? Can we manoeuvre
the bend? And what of that thin tube
of air, the only thing between us
and what we prefer not to think about?

BREAK-OFF

The hydraulics scream like a dry horse
as they tug-o-war with a steel trap
wedged into the cragged face
of a submerged cliff. Snagged up
at eighty fathoms, groundline
taut as a piano string, I imagine
the block busting off the davit;
keep seeing the poly snap and lasso
our skipper as it plunges like a loosed
snake into grey water, stealing his
hand or whole body to its lair.
What are the odds of losing a limb
or life out here? Who knows.
We hear stories, and close calls
are as common as hang-ups,
so just try to keep your head on
                              straight.

SCOTCHMAN SALVAGE

Don't slip. The bark's been skinned off
these cedars by the grapple-yarder pull
and tug-haul down the Strait: they're slick
as *umbilicaria* lichen after downpour; one mis-
step and the space between logs
will suck me under
and seal. What is it about risking life
to salvage stray gear
that enlivens? Stab the pike pole
into softwood. Inch near. At the front
crook an arm over the tow cable and sink
down onto submerged logs, water
vortexing my waist. One look back
to the boat idling at the edge of
the boom, then thrust the pole-hook
to snag the balloon's frayed line. Spike it.

BETWEEN STRINGS

Stoop against the portside gunwale
in a thin slat of sun ducked
under the deck awning, listen
to the wake wash off the stern.
Wish for a long run this time –
our limbs are tired, feet and fingers
swollen – long enough to rest,
watch the Sea-to-Sky steam train
whistle along the cliff. Smoke.
It's this lullaby of the boat's
slow roll through wispy chop
that lightens and sustains us:
as the main hums below deck
we watch our measured approach
to the next string, like musicians
anticipating the wand-wave to allegro.

SORTING

The trap comes out of the water
like a torpedo. I unlatch the drawstring,
thump the steel-frame base with
the butt of my wrist, and it all
dumps out onto the sorting tray.
Pick through the pile of clawing,
flapping bottom-dwellers like a crow
in a heap of garbage, only faster.
And faster, as the line whine-whirls
through hauler plates, toss overboard
box crab crawdad dungeness
cuttlefish shrimp black cod
like a bullet. Keep the legal-sized prawns
for the finger packers to drown and freeze.
No wonder Simon Peter was so ready
to believe God could be a man.

SETTING

Snap it on and the anchor scrapes
over aluminum, plunks down into
the purling wake. The line sinks fast
where it falls. Just past noon, our day
already old, but far from over.
I've done this so many times
that it's mindless, so I drift back –
my arms snapping on traps the way
automated machines assemble things –
to my first day on the sea: panic
in my muscles as I fought the line
zinging past my face, wrestled with each
knot that leapt like a crouching wildcat
from the line basket. Now I sidestep
their pounce, daydream as they pass
of all that becomes second nature.

GUTTING

Peel back the squirming tentacles
and slice the beak out like the stem
of a pumpkin. As I flip its head inside-
out, I can't help thinking *sentience*
of a four-year-old child, can escape
from a screwed-down mason jar, emotions
are displayed through shifting
skin colour. The dead, still-groping body
in my hands is dark, its sepia fluid
soaking into my sweater and gloves.
I bring the glinting blade down and
cut the blue-grey guts away, catch
my reflection in the steel-shaft
mirror: guilt-wracked, gut-sick
for two bucks a pound, fish feed,
tako sushi on Robson Street.

SOUNDER

The transducer eye half-blind following
a long summer of face-firsting chop,
the sounder screen is orange-yellow-
blue breakup, a stereogram image
that, stared into deep enough, yields
to clarity. Tired, I zone out, searching
for nothing in its indecipherable scroll
of crumbling rainbows, the false promise
of technology exposed, its glass face
sheepishly blushing.
                                    I can honestly say
I had no idea – having placed such trust
in my forebears, fashioners of the many
tools we depend upon for procurement and
pleasure – that a day would come when I
would sit, exhausted, and curse a machine
for my own inability to see the depths.

DRAGGING

Heave the heavy, many-pronged drag
over the starboard gunwale and watch it
slap grey water, sink. Somewhere
down there's a whole string of gear
clipped of its lifelines to the surface
by a tug captain playing connect the dots
with our bobbing orange scotchman. Fucker.
We wallow in the doldrums of waiting
while our skipper, eyes pinned to the sounder
and plotter, curses his luck and hauls up
something's rusted sunk something, old algae-
slimed groundline, a cluster of drowned
beer cans. That string's worth five grand, but
there's a limit to how long we can hope
for recovery, when each pass keeps
coming up junk, or empty.

MENDING

Black mesh torn by the rock shelf's clinging
resistance, its gnarled-tooth gnawing, this trap's
become a sieve all but octopus, Dungeness
and dogfish slip through. Between
strings I take the mending needle
spooled with green twine, stitch
the gaps the way my skipper sealed
the gash in his own palm
when a hook embedded in the line
hauled through his hand and ripped it open.
Everything out here is sharp-edged,
broken. Half our time working with holes
we've no time to mend. I take
each spare moment to tie frayed ends:
reef for tension, knot the twine,
and cinch down tight.

BREAKDOWN

Do you smell something? Diesel pissing
out a cracked fuel line, swamping the engine-
room bilge. Cut the main and slop down
into it. *Anyone got some chewing gum,
silly putty?* Northerly swells pushing us
powerless towards shore. *Don't light
that smoke ya dumb-ass,* the hull's about to
thrash fibreglass against granite and we're
four half-baked mechanics shin-deep
in diesel, guessing at bleed nuts, gaskets.
Clamber to the bow and throw the anchor
out quick, pray it will stick in the aphotic
mud flat, ease our panic while we wait
for response to our call. Anyone
to tow us back into harbour,
the dock, the still breakwater.

SPLICING

Three skeins of fresh line
unwound at each end into three
crooked fingers. Burn the tips
to wax nubs, intertwine. Dusk
sifting down through Bowen Island
cedars. Gulls perched silent on each
dock-cleat. Creosote. Cog grease. I fid-pry
the tight poly-spiral open and slip
a waxed end through, my stiff hands
moving to the auxiliary's hum underfoot,
the slow *slish* of slack water. Inside
the wheelhouse the skipper's cooking
chicken, other deckhands playing rummy,
smoking pot. The day's settling like till-silt
but I've got one last job to do: link
these skeins into one strong line we can use.

MORNING SET

In the morning the languid rhythm
of waves lapping the fibreglass hull
lulls us from dreams of softer beds
to the catacomb dark of the fo'c'sle.
The tired boat tugs its tie-lines,
bow, spring, and stern, then rolls
in waning slumber, groggy in its slip.
The creak of bumper on tire, the wind-
chime ringing of stabey-pole rigging,
even the gulls' off-key mewling
coaxes us back into foggy half-sleep –
till the shrill clang of the alarm clock
and our skipper's coarse, timbral cough
lifts the dream-load from our weighted eyes
and we rise to his footfall and Zippo-flick –
the whine and sputter of the diesel turning over.

SWIMMING THROUGH INERTIA

.

SWIMMING THROUGH INERTIA

i.

An aquamarine sky fathoms before dark.
Seagulls swim through currents of crisp air and smog
against the backdrop of Grouse Mountain's
tight constellation of energy waste. On Granville
vendors hawk junk jewellery by
the pale light of Coleman lanterns
to wide-eyed, pliable adolescents
who try on, sucker, and spend. The over-groomed
lineup outside the Roxy. Across the street
tattooed runaway kids slump in a huddle
hungry for drugs, a real meal to eat,
and something they can't quite name.

I'm sleepwalking home in a perpetual
dream one fluorescent awning at a time;
digital bird-chirps beckon me through streets
where the only thing surreal or strange
is how everything always appears
to change, but doesn't.

ii.

Rusty exhaust coughs an untuned transport truck
up Main, as Asian girls roll their bikes down

the sidewalk, talk in a tongue I don't understand –
about what, life in a city I'm trying to? A young couple

embrace at the curb then unlock
their Civic and zip into the slipstream

as a bearded acid-case barefoots it by
mumbling something remembered of the logic

that sold his life out to *freedom*, and two Salish women
saunter their big hips past, to-go

cups hoisted like talking sticks in their hands,
leather purses swinging where woven cedar bark would.

iii.

At Main and Hastings they freak-walk under
frenetic neon. Bodies reject bread, convulse
for want of heroin. Of course they're
human, but my fear writes them
off as AIDS-lepers: will not make eye contact,
wash their feet, slow my stride stepping
over some passed-out junkie's
body, could-be-corpse.

Crossing Terminal Avenue, exhales lengthen
muscles slacken. Venus in the midsummer sky
guides my good eye up, footsteps forward.

Walking this route home is exercise
in faith: who doesn't lose a little in humanity
each time their own weakness
overwhelms the impulse to compassion,
even decency?

Everything's shift: the open pit
where an Esso station pumped
a week ago, the McDonald's with its
green motif make-over, streetlights looming
like the eyes of something sinister, yet
comforting, watching over rows of fenced-in
houses where we keep.

GARBAGE STRIKE

Those idle nights we spent stoned and cynical.
Trash piles fermented in the heat.
The rot scent rose from stove-top streets.

Afternoons we picked through eastside alleyways,
Sally-Ann style kids scavenging
for a free shirt or lampshade, then cruised

past the picketers at city hall
honking and hollering in support.
Don't be misled, this was no show

of solidarity: we couldn't have cared less
about their children's dental coverage,
their wage demands and job security –

just wanted it to keep going,
pyramid piles of cat-piss sofas
and swollen Glad bags lush and growing

into back-lane fire hazards, sidewalk receptacles
cascading a ground cover of scratch-
and-wins, cigarette packs, and candy wrappers;

a scrawl of graffiti tagged across the city: *We are creatures
of habit, not reason,* a stain that's lingered
long since that season – those nights

lean rats feasted and fattened
as we scoured the city
and held our breath.

DUSK

Last light sweeping rooftops, already
the shade's incremental creeping up black-
red brick walls, over steeply pitched
peaks, a slender moment golden, now grey

squirrels scurry along storm gutters
above children rushing home from cement
schoolyards on bicycles, basketballs
cradled in hands bright pink from pinching cold

late afternoon, late November air exhaled
in white plumes from tiny purple-red lips
and exhaust pipes sputtering carbon
from cars and trucks pushing along

freeways, thousands of people locked in
flux, fidgeting radio dials, gas brake clutch,
sunlight receding as they pull into suburban
homes, a few precious hours of private

solitude or family time before sleep seeps in
to the rhythm of rodents rustling in walls
and beyond them the muted, distant cacophony
of all those still seeking shelter –

HOUSE FIRE

I did not have to turn to know that smile –
I'd seen it on my own face, I'd known
the same hump in my shoulders, the cold
gleaming in my eyes, and wanted not to see.

"Burned," Philip Levine

Manic in my underwear, barefoot, mid-winter
sleet streeling icy relief down the second-degree
burns on my face, I stood on the opposite side
of the street watching firemen extend a ladder
through the glare of whirling red lights, water
coming up hard from the hoses like the bile
from my stomach to throat, my best friend
standing beside me, laughing, as the roof
collapsed into a charred truss-pile.
I did not have to turn to know that smile –

that next-door-to-horror-is-hilarious grin
as common among young nihilists as sin
and its negation. As house parties carrying
on through the night, the neighbours kept up
by the blaring hard rock and raucous din,
too wary to approach the house or phone
the cops, the outcome in this neighbourhood
ranging from respect to violence, poverty
keeping everyone edgy, chaos full-blown –
I'd seen it on my own face, I'd known

that crazed laughter from my own mouth
as I emerged from the flaming house
and ran down the sidewalk to embrace
my stooped, weeping sister, her small body
shaking from the shock and chill air, and cradled her
to some semblance of calm in my familial hold,
the night hazed by the thick grey smoke
spilling from roof to street level,
our two bodies forming a single mould,
the same hump in my shoulders, the cold

contrasting with the heat in my skin, casting
my mind back to the waking moment:
a voice in the dark calling me out of dream
to *Fire, one flight up* – and I bolted
from bed, up the narrow staircase,
to the door that was barrier between me
and the backdraft that lunged for my face
as I flung it open and stood, framed
in the doorway, a riot of coiling red flames
gleaming in my eyes, and wanted not to see.

BUS STOP

One sits on a tattered blanket
beside his backpack and cardboard sign
which he has tucked away
for the night. It leans against
the stone wall of the bank:

Spare change for
beer, tacos and porn.

I snigger at this, understanding
in my way this young man, close
to my own age, who is not that far
gone yet: still a fullness to his face, some
body to his *Hey man,* in response to my *Hullo.*

The other comes down the sidewalk
as I take a seat on the transit bench,
his bone-thin face protruding
from a black hoody, the acronym
AIDS scrawled in white
across the back of his
torn jacket. He begins
to pace behind the single pane
of plexiglass between us. My ears
on his footsteps, my eyes

focus on the pack of teenage girls
across the street, the goosebumps
on the muscle boy's arms, the dull
racket of anar-kids bashing guitars
and drums under a KFC awning, the three-
minute interval between cruiser car pass
and cruiser car pass, anything to suppress
the thought of what he and I
may or may not,
now or in the future,
share.

BALLAD OF A CAGED MAN

You can only approach yourself in the second person.
That is how far gone you are.
Still you know the subtle difference
between flotsam and jetsam and feel
a certain facsimile of fortunate
you haven't collapsed into *he.*

A wrenched back
for weeks, the weight of your slouch
unbearable;
         supine, prone, fetal
in bed, in and out of sleep all day.

Intervals between dreams
you conjure the conscious
origin of despair, and there
in thought's sequestrum:
      brittle, sun-bleached bones
      once fleshed, plumose, avian.
With a sallow finger you trace the skull,
follow the scalp line down
to the antrum of the eyes,
sluice yourself in through each porthole
and let those effluvial remains encage you.

*

From my cage I can sing
of feather and wing
that carried me through the sky

With every seed that you bring
you will hear my voice ring
of the days that once passed me by

Hear in my tone
of the places I've flown
and all the sorrows I've seen

I ask nothing more
than this cage and closed door
and never to be set free.

ELLIPSIS

Eyes droop to asphalt waiting for rain
to freshen its dirty face. Moving is
moving in place. These days
low pressure gets under
the skin: blood vessels swell, throb
in the skull. Joints ache.

What's to make of this off-kilter life?

Thoughts all thump in iambic,
terns waddle on dry cobblestone,
and you write like a silkworm
spinning its brains out, a sentry
standing guard for nothing
but his post. Look:
some birds don't differentiate
between window and sky,
larger species drink espresso
then blade to yoga;
each passerby a dot
added to a long ellipsis
tailing the end of a compressed
sentence all adjective –

Spit. Decompress. Run on
in the direction of thunder,
wherever that may take you.

WHAT WE COME TO CALL HOME

So I pulled an all-nighter, lush on home wine and the perfume of a young woman, then set out on the 6:20 AM sailing with my cousin. One coffee on the Howe Sound crossing, three over breakfast at Troll's, and all ripped up on caffeine I had half a mind to blow off my plans and stow away with him to the Kispiox for an autumn of seeking Matsutakes under the loam, moss and pines – but being almost centless and waiting on student loan money it was a booze-botched thought. So I got on the ferry to Departure Bay and promptly passed out. Woke to the "We are now nearing . . ." announcement, having slept through the earlier "Coachline tickets to Victoria now for sale in the forward lounge," despite the four cups, and had to hump my three bags weighing, say, two sore kidneys, one love-gone-sour, and a dwindling hope that I'll ever find *home,* twelve blocks uphill in the late summer heat to the highway. Sweating pints, dehydrated, I cocked my thumb over the white line and quickly coaxed a ride in an old Nissan pickup. "Goin' just outside a' Ladysmith," which sounds good to me. He's scrawny and talkative, and sparks up a one-hitter right off, and I think, *Why not, I've got a long afternoon ahead of me.* The road straightens as we exit Nanaimo and in the middle of a long stretch he pulls over, says, "I'm turning to the airstrip here so good luck, dude," dropping me and my bags off in the middle of *Gimmeafuckinbreak,* British Columbia, Population: 1. Now I'm stoned and stranded with cars and rigs blowing by at 110, and the weak-in-the-knees feeling means I'm worried. Not a car slows, let alone stops to give me a lift, and Apollo's chariot seems to be picking up the pace as it races towards the mountain horizon; another hour and the valley will be lost in shade and I'm looking at a night in a highway-side cornfield wishing Stephen King had been born dyslexic. So I start walking backwards along the shoulder, thumb out, bag straps searing the base of my neck, and I guess there's something to be said for a little effort because a beater hatchback pulls off less than a quarter-mile into it. Now this guy is weird. Granted I'm high, so my paranoia motor is all revved up having already had a few loops around the track, but this guy kills my every attempt at conversation with vague one-sentence answers and keeps fiddling with something beneath the dash. I can't see what it is and the whole way down the Malahat I imagine a blade or gun and a quick pull-off up some logging road for a little struggle and sodomy. I'm rethinking my to-this-point unwavering opinion that vehicle ownership is mere luxury, never necessity, and the manic of the *Moulin Rouge* soundtrack blaring out the back-seat woofers has got me contemplating the leap, tuck, and roll, my fingers hooked, clammy around the door handle, poised-ready. As we pull off the highway to Victoria's semi-urban streets, his hand keeps busy pointing out the bagel shop where he works, his apartment building, the bar where he drinks and plays darts nightly, and I'm thinking rather woozily that a beer wouldn't be such a bad idea as he turns up the driveway of the boarding house I've rented a room in over the internet and drops me within fifty paces of my destination: bed.

WHAT KEEPS US GOING

A certain affinity for the *Excess*
        in youth is a necessary prerequisite
to a full life aphorism, and of course a laissez-faire

libido. Gets us out on the town,
        our lips ready to seal around
the first bottle we can get our hands on. Stuff it up

with cigarettes and other smokeables
        like someone forgot to pull the drain-
stopper on summer's grimy dishwater; like the feast

just goes on and on.

Did someone say liver-fire, HIV,
        aging? You know I always drink
my nettles, carry latex, and shit we're still young

so do we have to go there tonight
        while the moon is still waxing and
the pull of celestial bodies is propelling us into orbit?

Stiff back, busted guitar neck, broke. He's normally one to complain, so here goes: worse than broke with a twenty-five-grand student-loan debt, rising, a hankering for alcohol that gets his gallbladder pumping out bile like a dairy cow on crack, a growing sense he'll always lack that certain something, the fact, of course, of that sentiment's cliché, irony another vice he can't quite shake, the way he can only write some things in the third person, his six-month itch nothing seems to cure, his paranoia, despite five second opinions, that it must be more than fungal, his tumble from the helm back to creative writing school, creative writing schools, two towers falling repeatedly on every TV he glimpses, the impression there's more of these in most bars than friendly faces, the neo-conservative "changes," his course load, weak kidneys, credit card, the usage of *all* as modifier, of *like* in colloquial speech, the destination he keeps moving towards but never seems to reach, a $75 ticket for running a red light on his bicycle, that particular cop's predisposition to *asshole*, his heart palpitations, chronic headaches, oversleeping, the Afghani woman's voice on the CBC, the homeless man head-hung-down on Government Street – her weeping, his silence.

WHAT KEEPS ME GRINNING

Didn't pass an open restaurant for blocks
   and not a service station
in sight, see, I'd been juggling my bladder
   leg-to-leg for a good ten
minutes and the heat from last night's drink
   and smoke was full up
like a hot dragon-belly, my bladder ready
   to explode in piss-flame.

So I ducked behind a holly hedge and

Aaaahhhh.

Shook off the piddle and zipped up
to turn and see Mrs.
What-The-Fuck-You-Doin'-Pissin'-On-My-Winter-Pansies-
 You-Little-Punk
staring me down from her kitchen window.

(Now, granted I lack certain urban graces and,
being a man, have open to me options
a woman may envy in these matters, but
hasn't anyone in Victoria heard the old saying
When you gotta go, you gotta go?)

And off I went.

Night-hooked. Wired. Can't sleep. Single-cot creaks with each toss-and-roll shift. Flip to the cool side of the pillow won't do it. Nerves fired down through feet thrust from covers. Eye twitch, crotch itch, fever. Rise from bed, pace naked, finger the phone, dial, hang up. He dresses, dumps his change jar, scrounges enough for smokes, heads out. Crossing the intersection he sees the neon Chevron glare, walks past the pumps, enters the kiosk, and asks the attendant for his preferred brand. "Is there anyplace a man can get a good stiff drink 'round here this time a' night?" "Just over the bridge, six blocks." Exiting, he strikes a match – it flares out before the tobacco catches. Strikes another and hauls hard till it burns. The first drag is sickening. He hasn't the heart to walk so far. Stands stretched in the echo of distant sirens, airplanes, car engines, cat-cries, then walks back down the dimly lit sidewalk, past closed up hair salons, hedgerows. At the foot of the driveway he squints out over the gorge: a drizzle of rain patters the estuary's black surface like buckshot. He thinks of times past, how he'd have crossed the bridge, walked under the maples and practiced *Qigong*. Breathed, dipped his hands in the water, wet his face. Instead, he turns and ascends the driveway. The house is dark, the other tenants asleep. Lingering on the front stoop he pushes the butt into stucco, flicks it under salal. Lights another. The smoke chafes his throat, scorches the mucous in his lungs. The neighbour's dog strains its lead, howls a raccoon nosing a heap of tipped trash. The porch light flickers, buzzes, burns out.

WHAT WE COME TO CALL HOME

Sick and weathered with soul-hunger
the night is sifting
strain from silence, the night reclaiming
solitude: alone and not
alone, the stars somewhere beyond.

A short tether tugs you
shaking across intersections, over sidewalks, up
stairs, through a door, down the end of
a hallway to

a room:
books, a dollar-store clock, change
heaped loose on the bedside
table, a half-mug of cold tea.
You drink the dregs
and make one last attempt with pen and paper before
lie-down.

Outside, the night
is renewing itself.
The walls leak
TV-talk, water-whine,
as the second hand
cleaves the dark
like the tolling of an old bell –

  Sleep now, unstill I,
to the steady measure of seconds.

WHAT BRINGS US TOGETHER

Once I stood in a room consumed
by flames. They sprung
like coiled snakes from the walls
and scorched my face. That spring,
the north wind tore across Knight Inlet
and the cold felt hot upon my skin.

My world has been a confusion
of fire and water since. Speak to me

of elements. You have been
other places. Say earth, air, fingernails,
feet; where you have walked, praised,
collapsed like a burnt-out roof.
Find words for what is
visceral, urgent, and cannot be
articulated: where language ends
and we are left only
to be touched, taken, held.

WHAT SETTLES

Early morning. Outside the kitchen window stars
still visible in the blueing sky. Flip the switch

and the overhead fluorescent sputters, blasts
sharp light from the ceiling. Fill the kettle. Turn

the element to high and wait for the steam-
cry to rise. Steep two bags of jasmine-green

in a one-litre mason. Screw the rust-flecked lid
tight. Throw on an old hoody, cram feet in shoes and

exit the front door. Descend the driveway.
Keep sleepy hands warm against glass. Cross the bridge

and follow the path along the water's edge
to a small bay and thin jut of sand. Sit. Unscrew

the jar top, sip carefully. Watch seagulls
watch the water, crows cawing night's tail. Dig

hands into damp sand. Inhale kelp-rot, sea salt. Sun up
over waking houses. The estuary surface shedding

blackness like a steamed-up mirror, clearing
to reflect the same mug of sky, its many variations

shifting expressions which over time form
crows' feet at the edge of an eye.

SHUTTER

THE GREAT WAR MEMORIAL HOSPITAL

I got down on my hands and knees there
under a massive tired maple, cars slowly rolling by
over dry icterus leaves. Put my forehead to the ground
and slowly breathed.
                Having come hoping
to see the room I'd been born in, the room I'd been
rushed to, breathless, for incubation, I inquired
at reception: twenty-five years and the building
renovated, re-renovated, a waiting room
where the young nurse supposed
the infant ic may have been, the maternity ward
moved to a newly constructed wing.
                        So I wandered
waxed floors, patients and staff shuffling past, the intercom
occasionally crackling. Stared into the black-and-white
faces of soldiers glass-framed and hung
on pale walls. Read the memorial plaques, anti-smoking
and diabetes pamphlets, even thumbed through
the rack of donated paperbacks,
                   until I exited
out the emergency entrance, crossed over the asphalt,
and in the shade of that maple took myself
to the earth, those fallen leaves all around me.

HEADLOCKED

Bent and twisted brownskin/whiteskin
limbs entangled, stumbling together
to our knees, grass staining jeans,
you straining to overpower me, my
struggle for release: where
we found each other, skulking
on the schoolyard fringe, searching
for a porthole in –

My head just so
in the circumference of your arms.

*

On the days your hold clamped down
hard, you followed me, taunting threats,
home to the front yard
where I left you to sleep
in the woodpile below
my window, bedding down
with wolf spiders and wood bugs
a step up from the inevitable
shit-kicking waiting for you
at home. From the warmth
of my tucked-in bed I listened –
a knock, scratch, hollow thud –
as you settled your weight
to lie across the grains
of well-seasoned rounds
my father and I split and stacked
together in preparation for the cold.

*

The last time I saw you —
pissing on the fence
behind your crack-shack,
soiled jeans aslant
off your hips – a weary rage
festered in your face, squinting
in my direction
through alcohol and distance.

Over the stacks of foundation forms
I spent that summer scraping clean
and oiling slick, my choked voice
couldn't reach you
as you turned, swaggered,
and fell up your back steps.

*

I last heard your name at the bar in a drunk-
Indian joke. They laugh, say you've made it
all the way to skid row. Probably HIV-positive
if you're not already dead. I think of the few times
you showed up at AA meetings, sit back, try

to imagine you in one of those rooms
on the East Side: a cup of coffee,
muffin or cookie, taking a bite
with the teeth you've got left.

PINE PICKER

The forest offers this rare jewel
Matsutake button, its size
greater than your fist, white
flesh fresh as high alpine
untouched following snowfall,
the membranous veil still intact.
You are on your knees
low in salal
when you find it –
hands skim with delicate intent
over loam and moss until you feel
its certain density brush
your fingertips, peel back the forest's
plush green epidermis
and unearth it. Careful
as your father moved
when he taught this silence
to child eyes, you pick the mushroom
free from mycelium, remove
the dust from the stem-base

and lift a gold digger's grin
to the thick fir canopy. Taking
a plastic bag from your pack
you wrap your treasure in it
alone. All day you are mindful
not to load the weight of less-
valued finds above, aware
the thin veil rips
easily once picked. Evening
at the grading station
other pickers huddle round
the scale as you unload, watch
your slow hand
scoop into your canvas pack –
a plastic bag unfolded
to reveal
the most coveted of mushrooms,
the veil now slightly torn.

THE HAND MOVING

Where the light fails, be sure there will be hawks
Riding towhees or nightingales down through the dusk,
And one of us, in a dustcoat, waiting,
Seeming to understand.

"Cooper's Hawk," Seán Virgo

What music there is, cacophony of dirt and dirge,
won't come clean, lift: for her, fifteen, thin wrists
criss-crossed white for life, literature is a rumoured
world. What can I tell her, honestly? Writing will
not stop her stepfather's violations, cure her itch
for cocaine, her mother's frailty, won't lock
the man from her bedroom at night. She writes
My friends have all cracked, they scorch their youth
in a squalor-shack sucking rat-poison-cut-rock.
Where the light fails, be sure there will be hawks

and vultures ready to pick your bones. She knows this
and perhaps it is only another lie to make metaphor
from what's been done to her, what she's done
to herself: the criss-cross scars, the cocaine, her
self-starved slight frame. Life's a terror without
respite when through your days a rapist's musk
lingers upon your neck, cum-scent in your crotch. Can I
tell her there are answers in pages? That in Plath there is
wisdom, release? To relinquish to and trust
riding towhees or nightingales down through the dusk,

a simple line such as this to carry her from pain? Poetry
seems a lame, limpid animal in the crosshairs of real
despair: her downcast eyes' defeated stare, the soiled
grey carpet in this classroom creeping up her jitter-leg,
hunched, slender shoulders closing over her chest,
her fresh blood begging a fix, relief, pulsing
like the air preceding a prairie wind storm, parched
as the droughted land, the hand that slashed itself
gripping her furrowed face, caught between leaving
and one of us, in a dustcoat, waiting,

wanting to give her shelter she can't take, cowering
across from me, defiant, afraid. What I can know
of what she carries is nothing. Empathy extends
only so far before it falls in the chasm, thins
into air. So I ask her to write another word, a line,
to use the pen that shakes in her unsteady hand
to excise an abuse, a betrayal, a lie, any of the many
small deaths that burden, and in so doing do what
I can, reading the words she gives me and
seeming to understand.

FINAL MOMENTS

To hold the gun you used:
the grip of its grainy handle
the smooth, silky surface of
the barrel cold
as shiny coin.

To hold its potential against
a frightened bank teller's
face so tender, her fear.

Then fleeing, directionless,
winter air expanding my lungs,
blood coursing through capillaries
to each ecstatic, twitching muscle
the agility of adrenaline turning
somersaults all
inside

flowing smoother with each stride
through newly constructed subdivisions
past children playing street hockey
into the backyard of the city
under darkening wet trees, over roots, through creeks
then finally sheltering, lost
behind that dead cedar stump.

I would like to hear the officers'
distant voices
echo against the flow and
drop of nature –

to feel those final moments:
mind frantic, index finger stiff,
strong against the trigger –

raising that gun-fist against my winter pale flesh.

THE SLEEPER IN THE VALLEY

On a lakeshore lined with alder, maple, fir
where the leaves, having let go, speckle the earth
auburn, crimson, vermeil, the water's stir
turning low autumn light like wheels of mirth,
a young man, slackened, leans back, the soft leather
of his car's front seat cradling him in sleep:
head aslant against the window, hands together,
fingers intertwined, prayerful in his lap.

He is napping, a slight grin on his face,
having fallen asleep to unburdened thoughts
of the coming winter, his life's pace
slowed to this stillness, the knot
in his stomach unspooled like the duct tape
sealing hose-ends to tailpipe and window.

SNOWSCAPE

It was December. I'd never seen a sub-zero winter.
I must have been struck by the absence of green,
spindly trees thrusting branches of nothing
up towards thin overcast: a mirror

image of the snowed plain, trackless, without frame.
I can't say why it was I left the contour
of my huddled family watching father
lift a frozen coyote from steel jaws

and wandered into that veiled expanse –

Nor do I recall the crack as frail ice splintered beneath my feet,
or the gust of awareness that rises when life turns
precarious –

just the plow of my quickened legs through the snow, crust
   rasping against my knees,
and the chorus of cleft voices rising to the fore
calling me back to the familiar shore.

WHEREVER YOU ARE

Are you still hiding in the dark, curled
amongst medicine balls and tumble mats,
your wide eyes riveted to a shaft of sharp light
piercing the seam between doors,
praying away foot-scuffs on hardwood?

I am counting backwards
the days and years: ready or not
I gave up searching for you
long ago, left you tucked
in that musty corner you pulled me into
each time we fucked, love
locked out as we entered
the dark you could never seem
to emerge from, fettered
by the hands that found you there
and forced you open on the floor. Are you still

hiding behind that door, knowing
teacher will find you before I do,
his hands already moist,
his deep voice calling?

EMPTIES

Glass splinters on the kitchen floor –

she picks and pulls them
up off linoleum,
pricking her fingers on tiny shards.

The men have drained every bottle;
thrown the kitchen table down
sending empties, dominoes, cutlery,
the candelabra her grandmother gave her
to the floor, crashing;

stomped glass underfoot and slammed
out into a cold, dark
early morning,
into muscle cars, music pounding,
tires tearing frozen soil
driving away from her –

stooped over, suckling
on a du Maurier,
listening like an abandoned mother:

the inhale/exhale of her milling girlfriends,
the sucking whir of the heater fan,
the silence of the driveway.

SHUTTER

After you dressed and said goodbye
this morning, it closed.

I have been careless with my body and what I carry
are negatives developed to a blur.

This is what happens when one exposes too much – too often
the aperture insists you stare through it, then leaves you

white-blind. I have resigned my body
to images –

the way you pushed the screen from the window last night
to place your face into the rain,

the streetlight doing to your naked skin
what the moon no longer can.

THREE POINT O

Your jewellery box lid wakes us
to the walls undulating, the floor
swaying like a hammock hung
between them. The window glass
wows in and out and I catch myself
wishing for the Big One, *Come on baby*
prattling in my mind like some asinine incantation
as books lob themselves off shelves,
the asparagus fern nose-dives from the sill
and the stereo clicks on Built to Spill, drowning out
the dog's bark from the living room. We should

leap out of bed, react, be afraid, but

the look in your eyes is a startled wonderment
that swells my blood like I'm looking up
from the bottom of a deep crater
as the house settles back on its haunches
and I plunge into you, pushing for tremors.

LOVE POEM

There's still a scorched-stone-
liver in the larynx. I'm uncertain
if it's mine, yours, or the world's.
Some say there are those
cloistered behind walls
who've found an answer.
Around these parts this is hearsay
and so inadmissible. Perhaps
what we've referred to as love
is longing cloaked in fear.
This is conjecture. What is clear:

the outhouse pit's near full,
surface well's almost dry,
the creek pump's impeller, fried.
My back aches and I miss you terribly
when it rains, which isn't often. Somehow,
the snap peas and nasturtiums we planted
are thriving. I've gotten no call back
on that last job bid and Collections is demanding
a first installment next week. Sometimes, at night
I feel your absence leak; still it hurts less now
to slap mosquitoes dead
between my palms.

DOMESTIC ABSENCES

It is sound's absence I notice most: clink
of your knitting needles, creak
of your footsteps on stairs,
the flare of a struck match lighting
candles in the morning, sweep
of your slippers across the cold floor.

The starling's echo-call whistle
from the pines wakes me now,
the hens' impatient squawking.

I leave the CBC on low all day.

At night, the scurry and gnawing
of rodents on wood, not my head
between your small breasts,
the thump of your simple
heart in my ear.

The vivid tulips eat my oxygen . . .
and I am in that hospital bed
laid out prone
on this couch
in my apartment, my head
making its nightly note of the ache
in my chest – the crescent scar circling
my scapula, the one I've studied
in bathroom mirrors, my neck craned
back, constricting.

And I am aware of my heart . . .
tired muscle, anxious, tense,
as it labours to keep
a stable rhythm. Those memories –
needle, suture, sterile air, scalpel.
And before that, abrupt darkness
preceded by my infantile blood
flooding back from aorta down
patent ductus to atrium, ventricle –
all somatic: the brink
of panic: that vague, that prevalent.

What brings them to the fore: an article
in the *Globe* predicting a lifetime of meds
for infant heart-surgery patients;
a sudden violent thump against
my thorax like a wall-stud searching
for a hammer; a poet's words pushing my attention
inward, where my heart *opens and closes*
its bowl of red blooms out of sheer love of me. . . .

TWO WATERS

I could be the ghost of my own life returning
to the places I lived best.

Linda Gregg

i.

Sechelt: this *land between two waters* and outskirts the centre
and fringe of my world when bees in the grass were targets for
bricks and cars obstacles to play the daylong in sand pits and
salal whiskered rock bluffs walkie-talkies BMXs and everything
we wanted laid out before us any way we imagined the buzzing
monster power poles race tracks through yellow broom the moon
a pale-blue visage in the purple dusk as I rode the still streets home

Down in the shade-thick morass families stuffed mallards and
ducks with bread crusts and birdseed while we hid and sought
and fought branch-gun battles amongst the reeds and willows
detached into regiments and crept low hunting each other
without a tinge of hate in the heart or vaguest conception of
loss our fresh hunger a faint ache in the thyroid as we blew
each other to high heaven *bang bang you're dead* birthing
our first *who-shot-who-first* arguments

Shuffled through the blowdown after winds still receding hushed
off the strait playing at pioneers or prospectors the things we'd find
rusted-out junkers buried in salal empties discarded by the *Billies*
(old Indian winos) coyote carcass decomposing in moss everything
we'd come across collected and coveted in backyards and secret
hiding spots our stashes of loot weathered magazines burnt-out
batteries old coins fake jewellery we carried home elated mistaken
for gems

Along the long seashore unawares we stretched our pale-skin limbs in the sun salmon jerky scent wafting from smokehouses caught small crabs beneath overturned stones sifted salt-flecked beach glass from pebbles and fragments of oyster shell and seal bone lay under driftwood shade-shelters amongst retaining rocks as flocks of gulls and Canada geese bobbed idly on the green water we swam further from shore in each day the sea floor slowly falling away

New moon snagging salmon by flashlight creosote pilings creaking
black scent on the inlet air my first catch and cut into flesh there
the cold quiver of the kill come inside me my hands holding the
orange near-glow of salmon roe and the Indian silhouette saying
eat it, son the pearl-strand sliding over my tongue through my throat
then sinking the hook back under and lying stomach down on the
rough two-by-twelves to stare over the edge the old dock shifting
on the flood tide rising beneath

Pitch-dark shortcuts through thick stands of trees now fallen silent
ravine chatter and the rustle of wind or raccoons through ferns and
tall grass twitch of the sympathetic nervous system alert and aware
of each bending blade and slight whisper or scritch nocturnal eyes
trained on the faint light thrown by back-porch lanterns distant street-
light beacons guiding small footsteps through forests and fright
shivers down the spine and hairs bristling as I swivelled to squint
in the direction of each sound's origin

On mountain slopes made accessible by the blast heave and pack of logging road construction we barrelled up in a rusty pickup pitched canvas in the dusty grit slash-side camp amongst fireweed and willow herb mother cooked potatoes and pork & beans over propane burners while father whittled alder branches into roasting sticks beside the fire's crackle and hiss my sisters and I hungry and impatient swatting no-see-ums in the auburn glow of that first unsettling discovery

Hammer it dead we jeered pounding holes with father's steel
framer in every sheet of useable scrap wood he'd salvaged
stacked and sheltered from the sheer rain that sloped in on wild
southeasterlies howling off the strait popping clothes from their
pins the lid off the sandbox the playhouse door from all but one
precarious hinge in the aftermath morning the sun rose over the
as-yet-unmined mountain on a storm-dreary sullen-hearted puddle-
pocked town and father's weary admonitions stern and patient

ii.

I have grown to love slow things. The way seconds suspend
As the sun's upper radius sinks below the island horizon.

In the city I savour the screeching moment when the subway
Lurches to a stop, momentum turning in on itself, so time seems

To pause, just so, before the tritone computer chime
Sounds, the doors slide open, and the pace resumes.

With every breath, one less. I am thinking of the men digging
Away the mountainside above the town. The grey woman

Rests her wrists on the old piano, touches middle C
And sees blue; A, and sees orange. It is too much

For her life. In this world. The conveyor belt carrying
The mountain out to huge steel ships in the bay.

I go out along the spit in the windless night and bellow into
My own knowing and the still strait. Both behind and before me

The ships and trucks of commerce roar also, the rumble of steel
Flying through the high air descending. Trying to feel a space

Within origins and endings. The water on each side of me
Rising the incline of seashell and sand, flooding beneath my feet.

Returning wakes ghosts on every corner. Memories rippling
On the periphery of vision between clean new buildings

Floor to ceiling with gimcrack. Billboards. Traffic. Suburbia's
Low-swell panic moving in with each entrepreneur making

Natural Beauty synonymous with *Investment Opportunity.*
The small before town replaced by retirement, commuter, resort.

Heat from the gravel mine's night-shift industry hovers above
The town, ringing. TVs twinkling half-drawn windows. Satellites

Adrift across the open sky. Beyond the bay, American submarines
Cruise the strait, their bellies aflame, nuclear. In the distance

The city's perpetual fire casts its opaque light against smog-
Stifled clouds, too thin to let go and give themselves over.

Just as the first grey big-box goes up, the city begins
Relinquishing its grip. I watch a huddle of teens shift

Their eyes as the old woman carts her groceries down
The sidewalk, their restless feet kicking up nothing.

Encroachment making a burden of affluence and leisure.
I tip my chin and smile as I pass. Better late than never.

There has been too little rain so the salmon sway in the estuary.
The fishermen enter the water at dawn, their white skin

Beaming in dark blue air. I rise to the window having slept
Badly, my lungs dry as the land, the moon too bright.

A few moments now, in the cool dark, before the sun sets
Its light on the water, and the whole bay begins to shimmer.

To remember, I come to this last cathedral of millennial trees
Bordered in every direction by stumps greying in the open sun.

Far below, the conveyor belt churns continuous above trucks
Churning sand to cement for a new mall's construction

As I lie down on bright, unbroken moss, and listen through
The residual cacophony to the sound of water, settling and clear.

NOTES:

Some of the words used in "Night Haul, Morning Set" are, for various reasons, not found in the COD.

Aphotic refers to the lightless biogeographical region below sixty fathoms of water where any organism directly dependent on photosynthesis cannot exist.

In this instance, *fid* refers to a conical, concave, stainless-steel shaft with a wood handle, about twenty centimetres in total length, used when splicing line and mending gear.

Scotchman appears in the OED with the following nautical definition: "A piece of hide, wood, or iron, etc. placed over a rope to prevent its being chafed." West Coast fishermen use the term to refer instead to the bright pink or orange flotation buoys used to both float their groundline ends and mark their sets.

Stabey pole is common slang for stabilizer pole.

"The Sleeper in the Valley" is a variation on Rimbaud's "Le dormeur du val."

The italicized lines in "Rereading Plath" are from Sylvia Plath's "Tulips."

ACKNOWLEDGEMENTS:

Night Haul, Morning Set was originally published as a chapbook by Junction Books. My thanks to Carleton Wilson.

"Three Point O" originally appeared as a High Ground Press broadsheet. Thanks to John Pass and Theresa Kishkan.

Some of these poems have appeared in *Grain, Event, BC Studies, The Malahat Review, Books in Canada,* and *The Literary Review of Canada.* My thanks to the editors of each.

"The Sleeper in the Valley" is for Rob Denham, in memoriam.

"Final Moments" is for Nevin Sample, in memoriam.